Beautifully

Imperfect

Chai Passion

Friend...enemy...aggressive....passive...
outgoing...withdrawn...
loud....quiet....charming...rude...leader...
follower...wife...mother..
grandmother...sister...aunt...cousin...
I am all encompassing...I am everywhere
but I am nowhere...I see as you see...live as
you live...I cry...I forgive...I am
confident...strong...observant...I am
listening...I am friend...

I am CHAI PASSION

חי

Window Seat

Stop being a passenger in your own existence...you are the conductor, you have the right and permission to drive your own life. Stop allowing people to come into your world and telling you how to run your adventure. Everything that happens to you and for you is because of you. No longer allow people to tell you what is good for you only you know that. Your life a precious stone, a valuable commodity, worth more than gold and the moment you realize that you will start to have a shift in how you conduct your life. You will stop allowing people to stop by and lay their guilt and fears and anxieties on you. You will stop allowing the back talk from your subconscious to control you. You will start to go the other way, sway instead of walk, conversate instead of talk. You have such a big stake in this adventure so use it to your advantage and stop allowing them to use it for their benefit.

Chapters of life...

All I can do is sigh as I think about the different transitions of life....sometimes we ascend and then sometimes we descend....we approach some transitions with happiness and hope while others with sadness and fear...we embrace that which we think is good, embrace what we think is our ascension but really it is not it's another form of us descending because we are looking at where we are with just a different color...brighter but deceiving lights...we think we are on another level but we are not...we are in the same place with new paint and a chandelier...so we stay....then we start to descend...or do we...maybe this sadness and fear is needed...maybe it's for our best...maybe this sadness and fear is the catapult we need for us to truly ascend...to truly go further than we ever thought we could...we are now forced to tackle those things that we have buried but continue to visit and water...we have to ask ourselves do we really want to reach higher or do we want to continue to fake it...some truly don't want the work and sometimes pain that is attached with ascending because it is hard work along with new and unknown pain...pain that has no name and newness that is raw...so we continue to descend...we continue to embrace the downfall because on this path we know that pain...we know the work is next to none or it is familiar work...work that continue to congratulate ourselves when we complete it...but it is an empty congratulation because you knew the outcome...so ask yourself are you ready....

Cheat

You can't continue to cheat yourself out yourself...you can't continue to treat you as an afterthought...you constantly give yourself away to everything and everybody but yourself...you answer the beck and calls of everyone except yourself...you are crying out for you but you are choosing to ignore you...your life is starting to become unbalanced, unraveled and you wonder why can't I be happy, jump for joy, smile...you have to come into the realization that your life needs you...it wants to be pampered and nurtured...it wants you to wipe the tears from its eyes as well as clean it nose...your life wants to watch a movie with you, dance with you because it see you doing it with others...love on yourself...give yourself what you give others plus so much more...make you smile from the inside...tell yourself that you are beautiful...that you are strong...that you are valuable...you need you to be happy...you are waiting...

Death...

I have died a 1000 deaths so that I may live...each death occurred to lay to rest the ideologies, lies, traditions and etc I was living...from each death I arose with a newer, stronger, more beautiful understanding of me for me...no tears were shed because of my death...no show of remorse...just a newness and awareness of who I am...

Hostage...

As I went inside of myself today I happened upon a hostage...she had tape on her mouth and her mind...her hands were free but she knew not what to do with them, how to use them to remove the tape off of her mouth and her mind...she only knew what she was told...never allowed to find for herself...she was looking to be rescued...looking to be saved...she longed for her savior...her knight...but it never came...she was tired but not defeated...she was worn but not ragged...she had this strength that she did not know from where it came...she could see but was blind...could hear but was deaf...could breathe but she was dead...she sat quiet of thought...she sat in the moment of receiving...receiving of direction...she was not impatient...she was not afraid....and then it started to happen...she felt a rumbling inside of her body...the blindness was no more...she was aware of where she was...she could hear the sounds that were surrounding her but she was still dead...she would not breathe on her own...unsure of how...she sat quietly and heard a voice say that it is not that you are unsure of how to breathe but that she was holding her breathe...she was told to release all of the air inside of her that was of no good to her...to breathe in new air...new life...and she did...then the tape fell of her mouth and off her mind....she jumped for joy...screamed of happiness...she knew she no longer was a hostage but a savior....she saved herself...

Improv...

When you take the time and really think about it you will realize that life is improv. There isn't a script, you must learn to live from the cues of the universe. You have to allow life to be formless without all the rigidness and rules that those around you will try to impose upon you. We have allowed ourselves to live a life lacking improv, without true fun, risk or whimsical adventures. We have become people that is living a life of just being satisfied and we must find a way to upgrade that. We have got to cue the music in our live...IMPROV...laugh at the mistakes and smile at the faults...no one should live a routine filled, uneventful, improv less life...that laughter, smiles and adventure is waiting for you as soon as you start to IMPROV...

Force...

Walk your walk, talk your talk. Show the world, the universe that you are a powerful force, a force to be reckoned with...

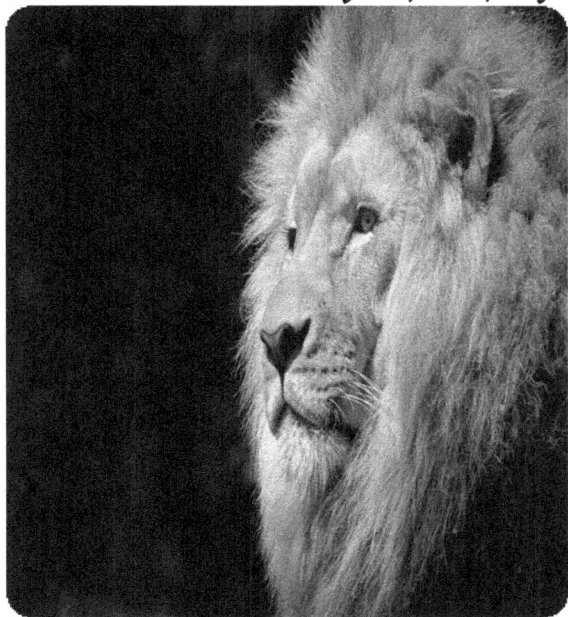

Living from the inside...

After years of conforming, giving in and complying the real you as gone inside and went to sleep. The real you felt as if it did not fit into your life because you no longer had a life, you had an existence. You have to learn to live again, how to breath on you own, learn to live from the inside. Allow yourself to be startled so that your heart will respond with a strong rhythmic beat, take deep, long breaths...breathing from the bottom of your lungs instead of those short, shallow breaths that many have become accustomed to. Get that blood to flowing freely all through your body and eventually awakening your mind. Wake yourself up and start living from the inside. There are dreams and ideas inside of you that are ready to breath, expand, live...

Learn to live life...don't let it live you....

When living life, you learn to accept and acknowledge the things you have control of, while also changing what you can and letting go of that which does not propel you...you can either be worn down to a nub or made to sparkle like a diamond. Life is unapologetic but sympathetic, full of rain followed by rainbows, hold you down in pain and regrets as well as raises you up in glory and victory. Life is a double edged sword with blood on both side. Blood of both victory and defeat...So learn to live in the sparkle instead of the dim...see the sun when others only see rain...smile just for the sake of smiling...raise your sword of victory...claim your victory...

Life in the key of me....

I have lived my life in the key of everyone except me...I have lived in family, friends, husband and neighborhood keys but not my own. I need now to have my sound heard, to live in my own key. I need for you to hear the soft roar that is me. To recognize my jazziness as I walk pass, to hear the sexy rhythms that rise from me as I approach or feel that gentle breeze bought on by the flute that plays as I speak. When I awake you can hear my tambourines as I sing praises unto the universe. During the day you can dance to my rhythmic drum that plays as I cook and clean. As I go through the day and interact with my children you will hear the sweet but stern sounds of my guitar the instrument that every good compilation has to have. But sometimes I need to be played, played so that my soft and sweet sound can sound like the whistling of a soft wind in a forest of trees. Play me, rub my strings, hold me closely, tightly but freely next to you as you come into my rhythm...

Soul Rain...

Soul Rain....my spirit is raining...it will stop
but I don't want it to...I enjoy the soft mist
and the dew drops as they fall....they feel
funny...they tickle my spirit...then there is
the down pour...the one that catches your
mind's eye attention...it doesn't have a
strong or make any noises other the sound
of rain hitting the emptiness inside your
soul...the raging storm is the one no one
wants to encounter but at some point
everyone needs...it cleanses you...removes
all that is not good...that has stayed too long
or is of no benefit to you...the drying out
process after the rain is so beautiful because
now you see...you see the purpose of the
rain...see the new, stronger foundation that
is now set and the beautiful flowers that are
blossoming...that strong tree that is now
standing...that strong tree being you...

Why you SPARKLE...

Because you defeated fear and replaced it with assurance...assurance that you have the strength to slay the dragon...

Because you stared down and overcame doubt...you found that courage and stood in it alone...

Because you found your voice and is not afraid to use it...you will no longer shut up or be shut down but instead speak with the roar of a lioness...

Because you overcame the storm that was your life...you told it flee storm don't bother me...

You are as strong as they come...your beauty and confidence radiates from the inside...you brighten every room you enter...and that's why you SPARKLE...

Strong woman...

I often hear people say of me that I am strong...I sometimes feel complimented or even a little confused because I then ask myself what does that mean to be strong....do they say that I am strong because of my response to things or the words I use or because I am not an outwardly emotional person...then I realize it is because of those things and so much more... I had to grow into this strength that they see...I had to fight both the seen and the unseen...I had to learn not react but to respond...learn words to say when responding...growing up I always saw so much emotional payment...I saw people use emotions to persuade or change things...crying, cussing, fussing and fighting are all emotional acts that I had to learn to remove from my life...I had to go through lack, decision making, wrong turns and dumb choices to grow my strength...I had to experience heartbreak in its rawest form to grown my strength...you see being this strong woman that is before you took a lot of beat ups and beat downs, cold days and even colder nights...I often felt like I was shunned because of my different thoughts or patterns but the shunning helped to develop my strength...I made decisions in my early life that the average adult would not have been able to handle but strength is what pushed me through...in strength building you will be ignored, pushed to the side and talked about but use those experiences as barbells, as weights...you will have to stand toe to toe on somethings, fight to the bloody death, walk alone in the darkness but you will eventually learn why...cry more than smile, happiness will be but a word to you...you will figuratively die a thousand deaths not knowing why...the road to strength is not easy but it is fulfilling...rejection from lovers and loved ones, friends and acquaintances can leave you feeling rejected...some people think you are born strong but I don't think that way...some also believe being loud when talking or having lots of words to say means you are strong but I beg to differ...you will be ridiculed and left alone because of the strength you have and the decisions you make…as long as you own it no one will ever be able to say you are weak…you will have to learn to manage your strength…not everyone can do as you have done, not everyone has walked through the fire without shoes on…don't allow your strength to leave you alone and long…your strength is needed because of your been there, done that, got the t-shirt way of living…

Synchronicity....

My dreams and my reality are starting to speak the same language...starting to hear each other speak...starting to see each other's point of view...starting to synchronize...there was a time when one was ahead of the other...one was speaking in a tongue the other couldn't understand and chose not to learn...they didn't vibe...they had to find a way to come together and make it happen but when dealing with determined dreams and stubborn reality it can be hard...neither wants to give an inch...neither want to submit to the other...ego was large and in charge...nothing was willing to intervene but then spirit stepped in...spirit went to dreams and spoke to it and asked the questions...asked what is dreams...are they accomplishable...dream responded and said dreams are deep thoughts that can only be seen in a quiet time and space...they can be accomplished by determination and compromise...then spirit went and had a talk with reality and asked him what is reality...can it be altered....reality responded with reality is what is right before your eyes...you can see, hear and feel it...reality went on to say yes it can be altered but it is a scary process because you have to start to look not with your human eyes but with your mind's eye...hear not with your human ears but with your spirit ears and feel not with your hands but with your heart...spirit then had to think about what each said...had to find a way to bring each one together without canceling either one out...spirit then went and bought dreams and reality together and asked dream do you want to become a reality or stay a dream that is never fulfilled...spirit then asked reality would he like the chance to start as a dream to be made into a reality....both had a bit of fear but also wanted the other to assist in validating the other...dream said yes he wants to be made into reality as well as reality wanted to become a dream...they came together..they started to speak one language...started hearing and understanding each other and seeing each other's point of view...they started to vibe...they were synchronized...

The beauty of the struggle...

The job you spent 25 years on has let you go...you come thru the ranks in the company, got awards and such...you thought you would retire from the company and then it happened..so now you are left without and identity or so you think because when people introduced you or you did it yourself it was always bought up that you have been on your job for over 20 years and people congratulated you...but now your think you will not have an identity...when in actuality now is the time, the time to awaken and live those dreams that were deferred or find something new...it is now time to do something different, not do the same thing somewhere else..but fear and ugliness is rearing its head...but now is the perfect time to step back and see the beauty in the struggle...now is time to go on the extended cruise or African vacation...you can start that business you have always dreamed of...oh the beauty of uncertainty...should you or shouldn't you...can you or cant you...yes you should and better yet yes you can...because of your struggle there is beauty...

No walk of shame...

Please know there is no shame in anything that you choose to do...your choices are your choices...no shame....spending time with someone you like...no shame...dropping out of school...having a child out of wedlock...no shame....we all make choices and those on the outside may not agree but that was your choice...never allow them to make you feel shamed because you did what you wanted to do or because you did something they did not have the strength to do...turn the proverbial walk of shame into a walk of fierceness...slay those dragons with their fear filled speech..show them you are not to be messed with...show them thru your fierceness...you are successful in your own way...you are the sunshine of your day...the light of your world...in your fierceness you will empower others...you will show them the road...give the map...make a pledge to yourself that you will not allow anyone to make you feel shame for your choices...

Lost my mind...

Lost my mind....one day I was walking down the streets and I realized I had lost my mind...I tried to retrace the steps of life to find where I had lost it...while retracing my life steps words kept appearing...they were in the sky and on the ground...hanging in trees and painted on walls...words like dreams, desires, knowledge, goals and compliance...I gathered those words and sat in the middle of the street as life walked by and just studied each word...felt good until I looked at compliance...compliance was different...it stuck out and it told me a story...told me the stories of how and when I lost my mind...it told me that I choose to comply...I choose to live the life that everyone else lives or told me to live...by choosing to comply my dreams went to sleep...my desires were stagnant....no knowledge was given or shared...goals were no more...comply...not a good word for me so I had to find a new word and it was independence...I had to make sure I had earned my independence and it not just been given to me...I had to awake my dreams and put movement into my desires...share the knowledge I had as well as search to find more...my goals were renewed and refocused...so I have my independence...I am free to live the life I want and never return to compliance...

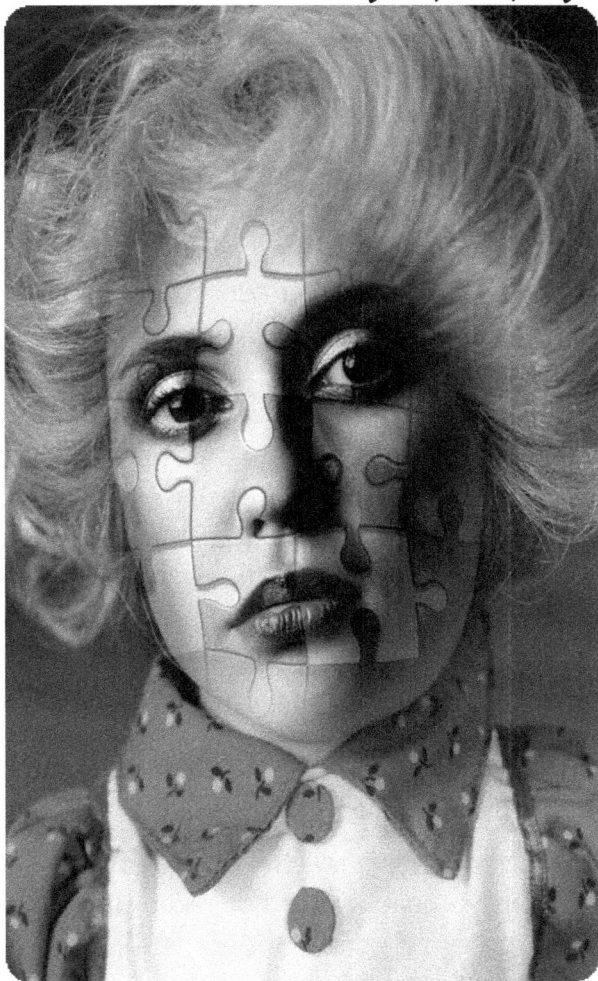

What does it mean...

As I embark on a new journey in this thing called life I am now pondering, asking the questions like what is life...is it a noun or a verb...who has it and who doesn't...what does it look like, taste like and feel like...you may answer with the typical answers such as life breathing so it is a verb and everyone has it, it looks however you paint it and the feeling is based on your own perception...I tell you one thing for sure that life is tricky...it keeps you guessing and questioning, it keeps you on your toes...life is not for the faint of heart...it is for the strong, determined and willing participants...you will cry today but laugh tomorrow, lack for a season and then live in abundance..life can buy you time as well as take it away...it is a teacher as well as a guide...it will teach you to hearken unto the quiet noises and gentle nudges while it guides you to your destiny...

Roses....

Prior to reading this book, you may have felt like a wilted rose; faded and dull.

But, after reading this book, it is hoped that you will feel like a beautiful rose; full of life, beautiful and strong...

www.ingramcontent.com/pod-product-compliance
Lightning Source LLC
Chambersburg PA
CBHW060102050426
42448CB00011B/2593